THE SIOUX

by Robert Nicholson

Editorial Consultant: Ben Burt,
Museum of Mankind, British Museum

TWO-CAN

First published in Great Britain in 1992 by
Two-Can Publishing Ltd
27 Cowper Street
London EC2A 4AP
in association with
Scholastic Publications Ltd

Copyright © Two-Can Publishing Ltd, 1992
Text © Robert Nicholson, 1992
Edited by Claire Watts
Designed by Fionna Robson
Story by Claire Watts

Printed and bound in Hong Kong

2 4 6 8 10 9 7 5 3 1

British Library Cataloguing in Publication Data
Nicholson, Robert
The Sioux . – (Jump! history series (2))
I. Title II. Series
305.897

PBK ISBN: 1-85434-166-9
HBK ISBN: 1-85434-163-4

Photographic credits:
The Ancient Art and Architecture Collection: p.30 (tr), p.31 (bl); The Bridgeman Art Library: p.9 (r), p.31 (br);
Edinburgh University Library: p.32; Mary Evans Picture Library; p.24, p.30 (bl);
Paul Harris: p.6, 7; By Courtesy of the Trustees of the Victoria and Albert Museum: p.19;
Weidenfeld & Nicholson Ltd; p.11, p.31 (t); D C Williamson, London: pp. 16-17.

Illustration credits: Maxine Hamil: cover, p.25-29; Rosemary Murphy: P.4-24

Contents

All words marked in **bold** can be found in the glossary.

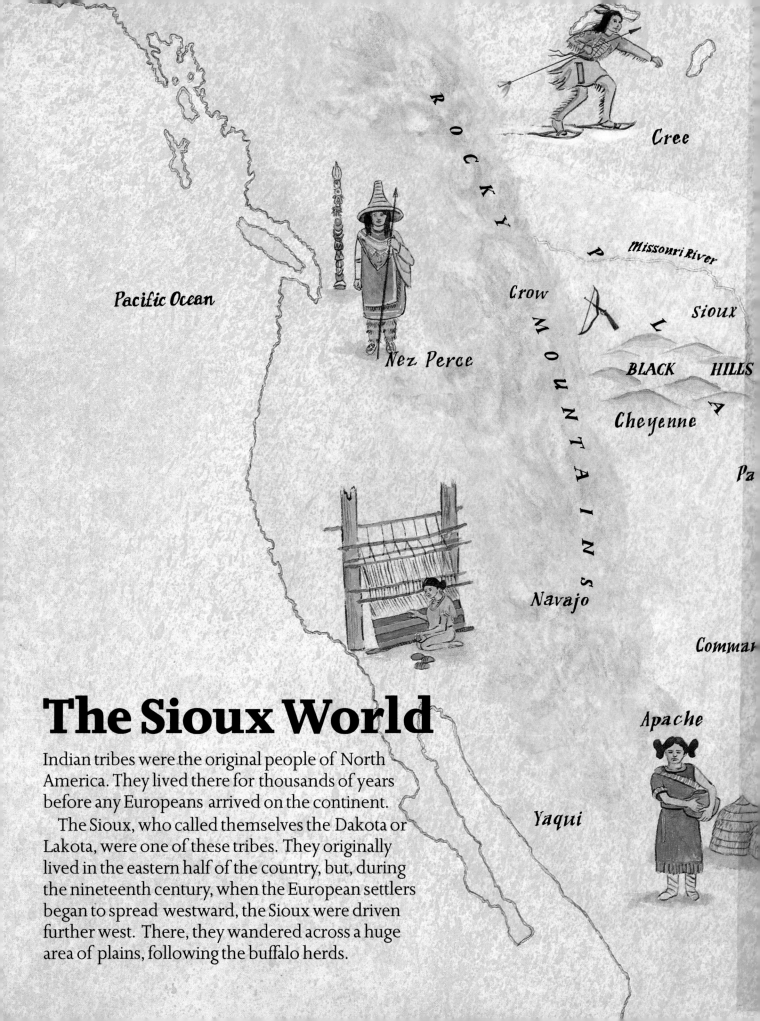

R O C K Y

Cree

Missouri River

Crow

Sioux

Pacific Ocean

M O U N T A I N S

BLACK   HILLS

Cheyenne

Nez Perce

Pa

Navajo

Commar

Apache

Yaqui

The Sioux World

Indian tribes were the original people of North
America. They lived there for thousands of years
before any Europeans arrived on the continent.

   The Sioux, who called themselves the Dakota or
Lakota, were one of these tribes. They originally
lived in the eastern half of the country, but, during
the nineteenth century, when the European settlers
began to spread westward, the Sioux were driven
further west. There, they wandered across a huge
area of plains, following the buffalo herds.

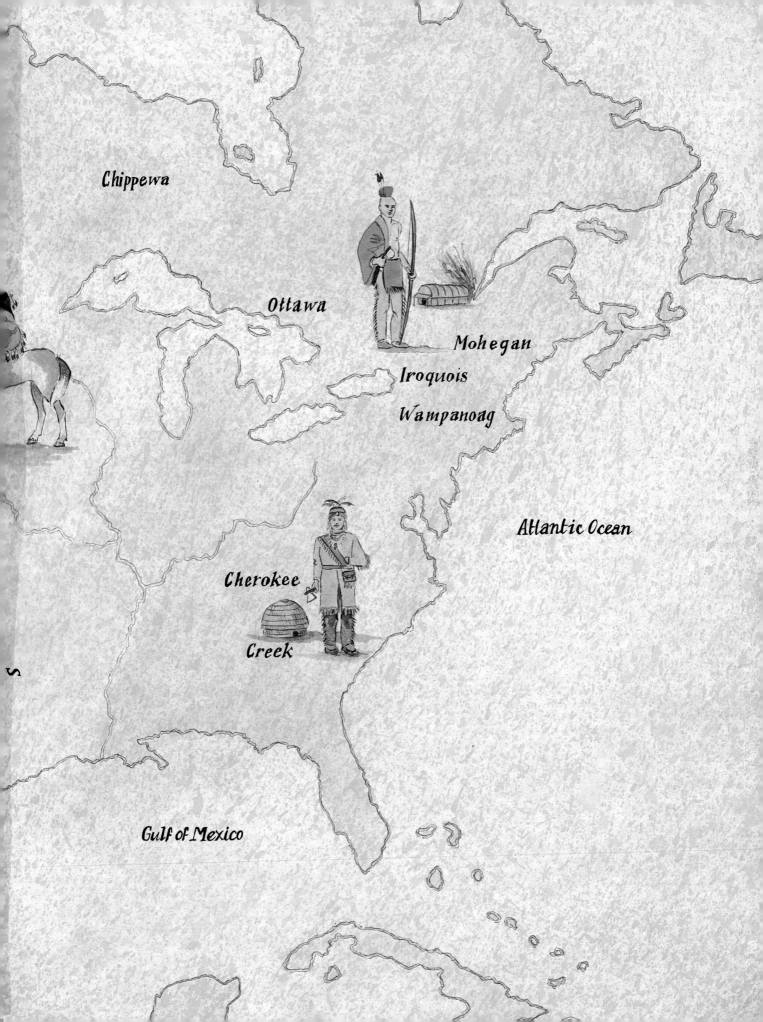

Chippewa

Ottawa

Mohegan

Iroquois

Wampanoag

Atlantic Ocean

Cherokee

Creek

Gulf of Mexico

S

Sioux Lands

The Great Plains area was very important to the Sioux. It gave them everything they needed to live – food, shelter and water from its rivers. The Great Plains also provided plenty of space and freedom for the Sioux to move about and to hunt and fight as they pleased. Together with buffalo, many other animals shared the plains too, such as coyotes, wolves, hares and foxes. Antelopes, deer and bears lived on the plains and up in the hills.

The Sioux valued the land highly and realised how much they depended on it for their nomadic way of life. They believed that, when they moved camp, it was important to leave the places where they had been just as they had found them.

Buffalo and Horses

The buffalo was the most important of the animals that the Sioux hunted. Millions of buffalo roamed the plains, providing a constant supply of food and other materials.

The buffalo skin was a very important material, but a lot of hard work was needed to prepare it for use. Firstly, the skin was stretched tight on stakes. Scrapers were used to remove any flesh and hair left on the skin, leaving the hide smooth. The hide was then rubbed with a mixture of liver, fat and brains to keep it soft and pliable, and then rinsed in a stream. Finally, it was softened by being pulled back and forth through a wooden loop.

▲ The American buffalo or bison has long, shaggy black hair covering its head and shorter brown hair over the rest of its body.

▼ Heavy loads were carried on special sledges called **travois**. Before horses were introduced, the Sioux used small travois pulled by dogs or people. Horses could pull larger loads much more quickly.

Shunka Wakan

The Sioux called their horses **shunka wakan**, which means sacred dogs. Before the Spanish settlers brought horses to North America in the seventeenth century, the Sioux only had dogs. Horses could carry much bigger loads than dogs and were much faster, enabling people to follow the buffalo herds over much greater distances. They also made hunting buffalo much easier and more exciting because hunters could chase the buffalo and shoot them from horseback. Horse stealing became a common reason for fighting another tribe.

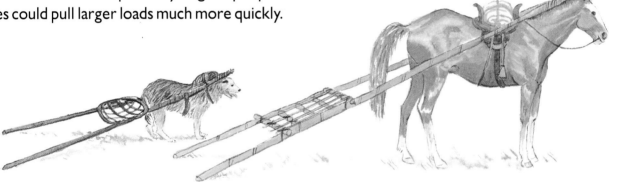

Horn, Hide and Meat

The Sioux made use of every scrap of the buffalo.
● Horn was used to make spoons.
● Bones could be used as knives or scraping tools to clean hides.
● A bladder made a good food bag.

● Skins or hides were sewn together for tents, storage bags and clothing.
● A skull was often painted and used in religious ceremonies.
● All the different parts of buffalo meat were eaten.

Making War

There were several other tribes of Indians on the plains. Some were friends of the Sioux like the Cheyenne and some were enemies like the Pawnee. The different tribes often fought one another. They were not trying to steal land or conquer another tribe. The idea was to prove their bravery. Many feuds between tribes went on for years, as each tribe sought revenge for the latest enemy attack.

Sometimes the warriors did not even try and kill each other. Instead they **counted coup**. They believed that getting close enough to an enemy to be able to touch him with a hand or a coup stick was much braver than killing him from a distance with an arrow or a bullet.

Signals

All the tribes spoke different languages. They could communicate with one another using a system of hand signals.

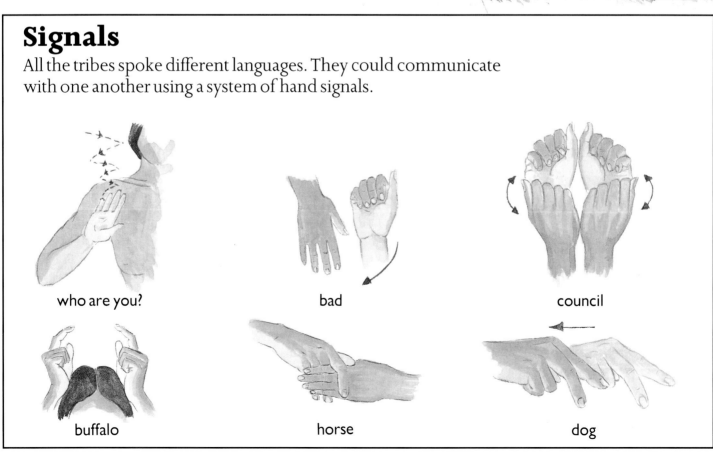

who are you?

bad

council

buffalo

horse

dog

▲ A coup stick, like this one, was decorated with feathers, beads and hair.

Heroes

The Sioux who are remembered today became famous during the Indian Wars (see page 24). These leaders united tribes who had never before acted together, in the struggle to protect their lands.

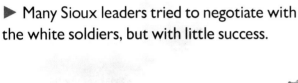

► Many Sioux leaders tried to negotiate with the white soldiers, but with little success.

Crazy Horse

Crazy Horse was a Sioux leader who refused to leave the plains to the white man. When offered money for the Black Hills, or **Paka Sapa**, he said: "One does not sell the earth upon which the people walk."

Sitting Bull

Sitting Bull was chief of the Hunkpapa Sioux. He struggled for thirty years as a warrior and leader to preserve his people's lands.

Red Cloud

Red Cloud was chief of the Oglala Sioux. He kept the white man out of the sacred Black Hills for ten years, but was finally forced to accept life on a **reservation**.

Sioux Names

Indian children were not given names when they were born. Instead, they were known by nicknames. Sitting Bull was known as *Hunkesni* which means *slow*. Some Indians won their names by performing acts of bravery and some were told their names by spirits in dreams.

The Tribe

The Sioux were the biggest tribe of Indians on the plains, and were divided into several smaller bands. These are known by different names, such as the Hunkpapa Sioux and the Brulé Sioux. Each band would split into small groups in winter, when food was scarce. In the summer, the groups from each band met at the summer **hoop**. There all the chiefs told each other what they had been doing, where they had hunted and who they had fought.

Each group was made up of several families who were related to one another. They had a chief who was the leader of the group. The chief could not force anyone to do anything they did not want to do. Above all, the Sioux regarded themselves as individuals, free to do as they pleased.

There were no laws among the Sioux. Instead a series of customs were taken as the guide to how people should behave.

unters and Scouts

Not all the men were warriors. In fact a few men did not fight at all. Some men were great hunters and knew all the tricks for hunting buffalo. Others were expert scouts and helped the band find buffalo or enemies. The man with the best memory was given the job of recording on a big buffalo skin what had happened to the tribe each year. Some men were camp comedians, and told jokes and wore funny clothes.

Women

Women looked after the camp while the men were out hunting and fighting. They would cook food, find wood, collect wild vegetables and make clothes. A small number of women went out fighting and hunting.

Men usually had only one wife, though it was quite acceptable to have more. Most women did not mind if their husband had other wives because it meant that they had less work to do.

Religion

Religion was an everyday part of Sioux life. The people worshipped spirits who represented the sun, the earth, the sky and everything else in the world. The Sioux believed that everything was controlled by the **Wakan Taka** or Great Spirit. It was the Great Spirit which allowed them to live on his land. Each tribe had at least one **Wapiya** or medicine man who could foresee the future, advise the tribe on religious matters and often heal wounds too.

Religious festivals took place at several times throughout the year. There was dancing and chanting, usually to a particular spirit. Dreams and visions were thought very important, as they were a way of communicating with spirits and obtaining their protection.

The **Sun Dance** was the most important festival. Men fasted for several days. They pinned their bodies with wooden stakes to a pole in the middle of the summer camp in the hot midday sun, hoping to have a vision. They believed that this would make Wakan Taka shine his light on them for another year.

▲ Each man had a pipe which he filled with bark or herbs. When a friend visited, the pipe would be lit and the men would smoke together. The smoke from different herbs was thought to be sacred.

Sweat Lodges

Sweat lodges were used for a religious ritual. Water poured on red hot stones created steam. The Sioux believed the heat purified and strengthened them.

The Lodge

Life in the **lodge** or tepee was ordered extremely well. Everyone had their own place to sit, work and sleep. It was bad manners to walk between the fire and other people – you had to move round behind them instead.

Building the Lodge

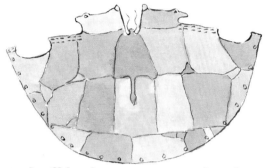

● 25 buffalo skins sewn together formed the outside of the lodge.

● Long poles were lashed together with sinew.

Outside poles supported smoke flaps which could be closed in winter.

The lodge was decorated with painted patterns or pictures of animals.

The fire was the focus of the lodge.

The husband's back rest

The wife's pots and cooking materials.

▼ Children often made their own toys, but more elaborate toys, like this doll, would have been made by an adult.

Children

The Sioux thought that children were very important because they were the future of the tribe. They treated their children with great care and seldom punished them. The worst punishment was having cold water poured on you.

Boys and girls learnt to ride when very young and by the age of six or seven were expert riders. By then, the girls would help the women with their chores, and the boys would be taught by the old men of the tribe how to herd horses. There was no school, so children learnt about what they would have to do as adults by trying to do it.

Children had plenty of time for games. These would often be races, mock battles on horseback and other rough games. In winter, they made toboggans and went sledging.

▶ Babies were strapped to their mother's or grandmother's backs on slings made from leather and wood.

The floor was covered with rugs made from hide.

Food

The Sioux did not grow their own crops or breed their own livestock, apart from their horses. Their food came almost entirely from the buffalo and wild plants which were all around them on the prairie.

The buffalo provided fresh meat, which was roasted or boiled in rich stews. It could also be cut into strips, dried and preserved to eat later. The Sioux also mixed it with fat and berries to make **pemmican**, a sort of emergency food to use when they were travelling or in winter when meat was scarce. Antelope and elk meat were also eaten.

Wild vegetables like turnips and berries were used to flavour meat and added to the rich stews. Most Sioux women kept a pot of stew on the fire to offer to any visitors.

▲ Before the European settlers brought metal pots, the Sioux used buffalo stomachs to cook stew. Hot stones from the fire were placed in the stew to heat it.

Clothes

The Sioux wore very simple clothes every day, but they had more elaborately decorated clothes to wear for special occasions, such as battles or ceremonies.

Men wore shirts and leggings and women wore loose dresses. Everyone had full-length robes made out of a whole buffalo skin to wear on top. On their feet they wore **moccasins**, made from buffalo skin.

In winter, these clothes would be worn under warm thick bear skins, cloaks and full-length leggings.

On special occasions, successful warriors wore feathers in their headbands. Enemy **scalps** were sewn on to a warrior's costume to show his achievements. Warriors and hunters painted their faces and the bodies of their horses with bright colours and striking designs which were thought to encourage the support of important spirits.

Decoration

Sioux women were expert at decorating moccasins, clothes and lucky charms. They used paint or porcupine quills, which were hollow and so could be cut up and sewn on like beads. Moccasins decorated with beads were often made as a token of love for husbands, sons or brothers. Feathers were used to decorate lances, arrow quivers, shields, **war bonnets** and pipes.

▼ A Sioux warrior had to perform many brave deeds before he could wear a war bonnet. When it was not in use, the war bonnet was rolled up carefully and placed in a long bag to protect it.

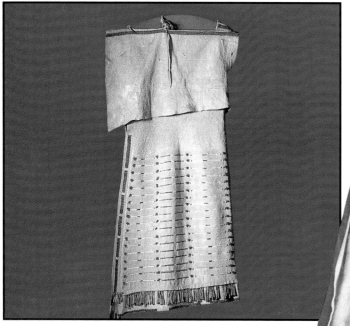

▲ Women would chew pieces of leather for a long time to make them soft enough for clothes like this dress.

Craft

Originally, the Sioux used dyed porcupine quills to make beads, but later they traded with Europeans for coloured beads. Try decorating some fabric with beadwork yourself. Work out your pattern first. Then sew the beads to the fabric one row at a time. Do not sew more than six beads with one stitch, or they will be too loose.

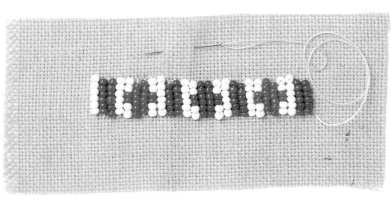

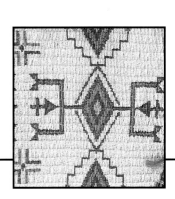

Feathers

Feathers were worn in the hair to show what a brave warrior had done in the war.

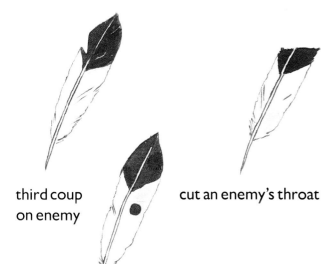

killed an enemy and took his scalp

third coup on enemy

cut an enemy's throat

wearer wounded many times

killed an enemy

fourth coup

fifth coup

The Coming of the White Man

As more and more Europeans arrived in America, they spread further west into the plains. They built railways, slaughtered buffalo and fenced in farms. Gradually, the Sioux way of life was destroyed. The Sioux fought for their rights and for their land. Although they won some battles, such as the Battle of Little Bighorn, where Custer and all his men were killed, eventually the Sioux were overcome by the army. Many Indians also died from diseases brought by the settlers, or from starvation as there were fewer buffalo.

Nowadays the Sioux and other tribes are confined to small reservations. With few buffalo left, they have learnt how to farm or are unemployed. Some try to live in traditional style, and make a living out of tourism. However, without room to wander, their old lifestyle has almost disappeared.

Buffalo Slaughter

● In 1850 there were 20 million buffalo on the Great Plains.
● By 1889 only 551 animals could be found.
● Today, because they are protected, there are about 15,000 buffalo.

The Crow Chief

The Sioux told many tales about spirits and about the world around them. This tale tries to explain why buffalo run from the Sioux hunters, even though the spirits were supposed to have created them to serve the Sioux.

The Sioux have always hunted buffalo on the Great Plains. Long ago, though, hunting was quite different. The buffalo understood that the spirits had created them to help the Sioux to live, so they were happy to be hunted. In their turn, the Sioux treated the animals honourably. They never killed more buffalo than they needed, and they always asked forgiveness for killing a buffalo, and then gave thanks to the spirits.

However, the Sioux had one enemy: the crow chief. At that time, all crows had dazzling white feathers, and they were very wicked. Their chief did not like the Sioux, and so he told all the crows to perch on the broad backs of the buffalo and tell them not to let the Sioux hunt them. Whenever the crows spotted Sioux hunters approaching the buffalo herds, a cloud of white crows would swoop down, shrieking at the buffalo:

"Quick! Run for your lives! The hunters are after you!"

At this, the huge, dark herd would stampede away over the plain.

After some time, the Sioux could put up with this no longer. The Sioux chief called all the tribe together.

"We must catch the chief of the crows," he said. "The crow whose feathers sparkle like the snow is the leader."

"But how should we catch him?" asked a woman who sat near him.

"I do not know," said the chief, looking round at the gathered tribe. "Someone must go alone amongst the buffalo."

One young warrior stepped forward. "I will go. I will catch the wily crow."

"You are brave," said the chief. "The medicine man will give you magic to help you."

So the young warrior went into the medicine man's lodge. The medicine man made a big fire with green, blue and pink flames. Then the medicine man dressed the young warrior in the heavy skin of a buffalo, and whispered magic words in his ear.

Outside the lodge, the tribe watched as smoke rose from the opening in the top. Suddenly, the tent flap was pushed to one side and a buffalo emerged. This was the young warrior, with the body of a buffalo, but the heart and the mind of a human.

The warrior made his way to the edge of the prairie. In the distance, he could see the dust rising as the buffalo herd approached. As they passed him, he joined the herd and ran with them. The buffalo did not know that they had a human among their number, because the young warrior looked and smelt like a buffalo.

On the ridges above the prairie, the hunters gathered, watching the herd. In the sky above the herd, a flock of white crows gathered, watching the herd and the hunters.

At a word from the leader, the flock of crows swooped low over the herd.

"Run for your lives," they screeched. "The hunters are after you!"

Bellowing with fear, the herd of buffalo stampeded. In a few moments, the prairie was empty, except for a cloud of dust and one lone buffalo, still munching at the grass.

The crow chief was surprised. No buffalo had ever stayed behind when the herd stampeded before. He swooped down towards the lone buffalo, screeching:

"Are you deaf? Run for your life!"

As the crow approached, the lone buffalo stood up on its hind legs and shrugged off the buffalo skin. Before the crow had realised what was happening, the young warrior grabbed its legs and tied them with a long rope. He tied a large stone on to the end of the rope so that the crow could not fly away.

Then he carried the crow back to the camp and took it straight to his chief. Outside the chief's lodge, the tribe was gathered round.

"You are a wicked bird!" the chief told the crow. "You have tried to break the sacred link between man and buffalo!"

With that he hurled crow, rope and stone into the fire.

As the tribe watched, the crow's brilliant white feathers were singed black as night. With a lick of fierce flame, the rope burnt through and the crow soared up out of the fire, and flew away, cawing loudly.

From that day, all crows have been black as night to remind them to steer clear of buffalo and men.

As for the buffalo, they are more watchful than before. If a careless hunter makes too much noise, the herd does not wait to be killed. It disappears in a cloud of dust.

How We Know

Have you ever wondered how we know so much about the Sioux even though their lifestyle disappeared so long ago?

Evidence in Pictures

Each Sioux group had an artist who recorded the events of each year on a buffalo skin. Each winter he would paint a summary of what had happened that year. This was called the **winter count**. It is possible to date these records accurately from the information they give us. One winter count, for example, shows a bright light passing across the sky, which has been proved to be a meteor that was seen in 1822.

▲ A few contemporary artists produced very accurate images of the Sioux. This picture by George Catlin shows two hunters creeping up on a buffalo herd.

The Popular Image

If a Western film is on the television, watch it carefully. Decide whether you think that it presents a true picture of Indian lifestyle. How are the Indians presented? Does it show accurately what happened?

▶ Some Sioux artefacts show images of the struggle with the white man.

▲ This is part of a winter count done on cotton. Can you guess what any of the images represent?

Evidence from Settlers

The histories and records of the Americans show how the Sioux were seen by their enemies. However, few soldiers or politicians really understood the Sioux way of life. For example, Custer claimed that the Sioux treacherously broke the treaties that they had signed. But often these treaties were signed by only one group of Indians, who could not represent any of the other groups. American records neglect to mention many of the times that the government broke treaties.

Glossary

counting coup
getting close to an enemy and touching him or standing facing him to show bravery.

hoop
summer camp when all the band came together. Lodges were arranged in a huge circle.

lodge
tent or tepee where a family lived.

moccasins
soft leather shoes, often decorated with beadwork.

pemmican
dried meat with fat and berries, eaten when food was scarce.

Paka Sapa
the Black Hills of Dakota, which were considered sacred by the Sioux.

reservation
a special area set apart for Indians to live in.

scalp
the hair of a defeated enemy which was used to decorate a warrior's clothes.

shunka wakan
the Sioux word for horse. A rich man was a man who owned many horses.

Sun Dance
the biggest festival of the year, when sacrifices were made in honour of Wakan Taka.

sweat lodge
a small hide hut used in a sacred ritual. Men would not eat for several days and sit inside the sweat lodge until they had a vision.

travois
a sledge made from two poles tied together with hide spread in between. This was tied to a horse.

Wakan Taka
the Great Spirit who made all things and allowed the Sioux to roam free on his land.

Wapiya
a wise man who saw visions and gave advice. Often called a medicine man.

war bonnet
the feathered head-dress worn by great warriors to show their skill in battle.

winter count
a pictorial record of the tribe's history.

Index